Leaders Working Together

Five Steps to Conflict Resolution

Robert S. Adams

Edited by
Katherine L. George, ABC, CAE

asae | american society of association executives

FOUNDATION

asae | american society of association executives

Washington, DC

Information in this book is accurate as of the time of publication and consistent with standards of good practice in the general management community. As research and practice advance, however, standards may change. For this reason, it is recommended that readers evaluate the applicability of any recommendation in light of particular situations and changing standards.

American Society of Association Executives
1575 I Street, NW
Washington, DC 20005-1103
Phone: (202) 626-2723
Fax: (202) 408-9634
E-mail: *books@asaenet.org*
ASAE's core purpose is to advance the value of voluntary associations to society and to support the professionalism of the individuals who lead them.

Susan Robertson, Vice President, Marketing and Communications
Anna Nunan, Director of Book Publishing
Louise Quinn, Acquisitions Coordinator
Jennifer Moon, Production Manager
Anthony Conley, Operations Coordinator

Cover design by Joyce C. Weston and interior design by Northeastern Graphic Services

This book is available at a special discount when ordered in bulk quantities. For information, contact the ASAE Member Service Center at (202) 371-0940.

A complete catalog of titles is available on the ASAE Web site at www.asaenet.org/bookstore

Printed in the United States of America.
10 9 8 7 6 5 4 3 2 1

Contents

About the Author

Robert S. Adams has 20 years of experience in conflict resolution and association management. He is founder and president of Rocky Mountain Resolve, Salt Lake City, Utah. He is also executive director of the Utah Society of Association Executives and the Utah Podiatric Medical Association. From 1988 to 1996 he was the full-time director of a 2,000 member professional association for public educators.

Prior to his work in association management, Adams served the mayors of various cities, including Salt Lake City, where he was chief negotiator, providing resolution to critical public employee disputes. During the 1980s, his experience as senior manager in labor relations for the Union Pacific Railroad provided the author with expertise and skills to manage a successful conflict resolution consulting organization.

Adams serves on the board of trustees for the American Arbitration Association in Utah and is a board member of numerous community organizations. Six national and regional organizations have appointed him to serve as a permanent arbitrator or facilitator. This combination of experience in association management and alternative dispute resolution has been a valuable resource in the development of this manual.

The author has addressed large audiences, conducted workshops, and performed board audits for associations throughout the United States. He holds a bachelor's degree in organizational communication from the University of Utah and an administrative law judge certificate from the University of Nevada at Reno. He is an instructor at the University of Utah and at Salt Lake Community College.

Preface

Associations throughout the world are increasing membership, expanding programs, restructuring, and for the most part flourishing. Representative organizations of every size and complexity are responding to the demands of a dynamic membership. Professional, trade, and philanthropic organizations are accepting the challenge of meeting membership's increasing demands.

Because of such rapid growth, the increasing complexity of these organizations, and the volunteer nature of most boards of directors, conflict of some nature is inevitable. This conflict, when short term and controlled, can be healthy. However, uncontrolled or extended conflict can cause the organization to become dysfunctional and might even destroy the very foundation of the association.

It is important to note that this guide is designed for both prevention and intervention. The collaborative problem resolution (CPR) model and approach have been designed specifically for use in associations. CPR is built on research from a cross section of associations—research that is intertwined with the well-documented, well-tested processes used in alternative dispute resolution as well as time-tested communication models.

CPR relies on the assistance of either an external or an internal facilitator. However, given that associations frequently pride themselves on being self-sustaining, the book also includes methods and a case study for using a facilitator internal to the association.

Simply stated, the purpose of this book is to help the association's chief executive officer (CEO) and elected leadership understand the diverse sources and consequences of conflict and to offer tools to manage and resolve conflict that is dangerous and disruptive to the functioning of the association—conflict that consumes valuable time and energy. Associations prefer to avoid or deny conflict because its resolution has been, to this point, a complete mystery!

This manual takes the reader through the history, development, and implementation of collaborative problem resolution for associations. Chapter 1, with its historical perspective, offers some insight into why conflict is so prevalent within volunteer and other membership associations. It also summarizes the key outcomes of the research project on association conflict that was funded by the American Society of Association Executives (ASAE) Foundation in 1999.

Chapter 2 describes the evolution of alternative dispute resolution—the precursor to CPR—and the terms, or language, of conflict resolution: disagreement, dispute, and conflict. Chapter 3 explores the process of CPR—its strategies, critical elements, and a five-step process, as well as the role of the facilitator.

The sources and consequences of conflict are outlined in chapter 4, along with the role of an attorney on the board. This last ingredient is intended to address the frequent (and frequently erroneous) assumption that having an attorney as a board member will either help avoid conflict or offer a free means of resolution. Chapter 5 sums up the discussion with measures to prevent (as opposed to avoid) conflict.

In conclusion, conflict is a natural aspect of decision making and can surface at meetings of an association's board of directors. Too, conflict is not always avoidable—often, it should not be avoided. This book focuses on dealing with conflict as it occurs and resolving it as expeditiously as possible.

1

Confronting Conflict

THE HISTORICAL PERSPECTIVE

A *Harvard Business Review* article titled, "How Management Teams Can Have a Good Fight," by Kathleen M. Eisenhardt, Jean L. Kahwajy, and L. J. Bourgeois III, suggests that "reasonable people, making decisions under conditions of uncertainty, are likely to have honest disagreements over the best path for their company's future." They further explain, "Healthy conflict can quickly turn unproductive." The real challenge is to keep productive conflict from degenerating into unhealthy, disruptive conflict and to keep a good team from dissolving.

David A. Whetten and Kim S. Cameron agree with the concept of a good fight. "Organizations in which there is little disagreement generally fail in competitive environments. Conflict is the lifeblood of vibrant, progressive, stimulating organizations. Dealing with conflicts lies at the heart of managing any business."

Zhiyon Lan, assistant professor at Arizona State University's School of Public Affairs, states, "American public administration in the 1990s has been particularly characterized by the amount of conflict with which it deals. The mixed functions of public administrators as conflict resolvers, observers, and parties to conflict often confuse public administrators themselves as well as complicate the public's expectations of them."

Lan further discusses the fact that most public administrators have not been adequately trained in conflict resolution yet find themselves forced into roles of mediator and facilitator. The court system then may become the inevitable last resort. The association CEO (that is, the chief staff executive as opposed to the board chair or chief elected official) is routinely faced with resolving disagreements and conflicts within the association, whether or not he or she has had training in this area.

Although the research resulting from this ASAE Foundation grant focuses on professional trade and philanthropic organizations, the benefits will apply to school boards, foundations, and similar board-governed volunteer organizations as well as their formal committees.

Professional organizations typically serve as the cornerstone of their members' professional training and networking, providing them with a singular ability to communicate with their peers and to grow within their professions. When there are barriers to effective communication between the association's membership, management, and board (in any combination), the entire organization may suffer.

Resolved conflict within an association is likely to result in increased productivity and enhanced member services. On the other hand, unresolved conflict can be all-consuming for CEOs because it redirects their energy from productive activities to reactionary management.

THE EVOLUTION OF ASSOCIATIONS

Professional, trade, and philanthropic associations have evolved from social groups to groups oriented to the protection of rights and upward career mobility. Consequently, associations of every type and size have seen significant changes in their leadership, accountability, structure, and purpose.

Budgetary constraints, government regulations, and competition from nonprofits and for-profit organizations are but a few of the crucial issues facing today's board. This discussion provides a framework for understanding why conflict seems to be more of an issue than it was in previous times. At least today we are somewhat less reluctant to deny the existence of disputes and disagreements.

The dynamism and vitality of a successfully evolving association depends on its collective ability to confront and handle any dispute regardless of size or complexity.

THE BREEDING GROUND FOR CONFLICT

The very dynamic of a volunteer board of directors presents an opportunity for conflict. Association CEOs have found value in healthy conflict, but, unfortunately, many have witnessed the destructive problems that accompany se-

SEVEN PRINCIPLES IN ASSOCIATION CONFLICT

The CEO, board chair, and board can benefit greatly from recognizing the validity of these principles:

- Conflict can be a productive and healthy component of the decision-making process.
- Conflict cannot be ignored or avoided as a means of resolution.
- Conflict can be destructive to growth, decision making, and the stability of the board.
- Any dysfunctional lines and styles of communication must be addressed and modified.
- Volunteer boards are an ideal environment for disruptive disputes and avoidance.
- Association executives and the board find that time is actually saved by making (even if it means negotiating) a commitment to conflict resolution.
- Leadership training should include a conflict resolution process.

rious unresolved conflict. The thought of full-blown conflict and a warring board strikes fear and dread in the heart of the sturdiest association leaders.

The research project leading to this book was designed to address the issue of conflict within an association's board of directors and executive leadership. Collaborative problem resolution (CPR) includes elements of both prevention and conflict resolution. Awareness of the potential for conflict, the identification of sources of conflict, and understanding the potential impact on association management are invaluable preventive measures. The CPR model serves as a set of tools for handling conflict in any volunteer board setting. The theoretical model lays the foundation for a logical and timely resolution process, given that the board has a limited amount of time to deal with conflict resolution in view of the larger agenda. Thus, this manual complements board and leadership training programs.

When dissatisfaction and even overt hostility surface in an association, it is typical that those involved are unable to objectively understand the motivations and source of the conflict. This is especially true in associations that encourage strong membership participation in business and management. That is why chapter 5 includes a self-audit that will help determine when conflict is unproductive and requires resolution.

The CPR process was designed as a model for self-intervention for the CEO, chief elected officer, and board members. The model does not replicate the alternative dispute resolution (ADR) process, rather it is an early intervention step designed to fit the specific needs of CEOs and volunteer boards and directors of professional, trade, and philanthropic organizations. While using the structure and format of ADR, CPR imposes and integrates techniques used in models of effective communication.

CONCLUSIONS FROM THE PROJECT RESEARCH

Five significant factors surfaced during the research process for this manual and guide. These perspectives, derived from the survey interviews and consultation, may be synthesized as follows.

1. **Perception is a problem.** Association leaders tend to believe that any form of conflict is a failure, and they view admission of conflict as a blemish on the integrity of the association's CEO and board or the strength of the association. Unfortunately, perception often becomes reality.

2. **Time is precious.** Board members are volunteering their time, which means they are taking time from their career, family, or recreation to serve on the board. Time cannot be wasted because of a lack of organization. In the long run, time spent on conflict prevention or resolution helps the board be more effective in addressing the entire program of work.

3. **Resolving disputes is a priority but dispute resolution is not.** Association leaders agree that disputes have and will occur as a natural part of the decision-making process. That does not mean, however, that they immediately welcome a formal dispute resolution process. Therefore, it is important to simplify the model, converting it to a user friendly, time-sensitive process.

4. **Dysfunctional conflict among associations is not unique.** Sources of conflict among associations are common; however, boards and their directors are diverse in their dynamics, purposes, relationships, and so on.

5. **Effective communication is a key to effective conflict prevention and resolution.** Obviously, the nexus of the board meeting is to communicate with each other. The constructive sharing of opinions is a basic factor in the decision-making process. The surveys identified lack of com-

munication or ineffective communication as a major instigator of conflict. Board members should assist each other in promoting effective
communication. This short primer can be mailed with the upcoming
meeting notice. Then at the meeting, the facilitator can allot 10 minutes
to sharing a few ideas on communicating with each other as a group.

2

Understanding the Language of Conflict

THE EVOLUTION OF CONFLICT RESOLUTION

The practice and need for conflict resolution has evolved over time. In the early 1900s, the growth of business in America demanded the need for professional decision-making procedures. Workers were demanding a participatory voice during the rampant growth of industry. Management desperately needed a model to resolve disputes and labor management needed a mechanism for presenting issues of paramount concern.

In 1925, business leaders in New York founded the American Arbitration Association as a clearinghouse for resolving business-related disputes. The nonprofit association has grown throughout the world to resolve disputes through mediation, fact-finding, and arbitration.

The ADR process has become a successful tool in resolving a broad spectrum of conflicts, such as family disputes, landlord-tenant differences, civic dissonance, insurance claims, civil rights issues, and medical matters. Municipal, county, state, and federal governments have authorized the timely resolution of disputes on local and national levels. Examples include neighborhood mediation ordinances, mandatory mediation in child custody disputes, and creation of the Administrative Dispute Resolution Act of 1990 (PL 101-552).

The most recent refinement in the area of ADR is referred to as collaborative problem solving (CPS). Its practitioners have drawn from the extensive literature and applications of ADR and contemporary management, leadership, and strategic planning theories. This process has brought about basic conceptual changes among the participants, such that there are no longer winners and losers, only collaborative outcomes.

Innovative ADR practitioners are endorsing and providing training in the new concept of CPS. The nonthreatening nature of these tools makes it an ideal choice on which to build the association management process of CPR. The cornerstone assumption remains: Collaboration does not mean we all have to agree, but we do have to maintain mutual understanding.

THE LANGUAGE OF CONFLICT RESOLUTION AND ALTERNATIVE DISPUTE RESOLUTION

The terms surrounding conflict are often misused if not also abused. It is much easier to understand concepts, theories, and processes if there is a common understanding of the terms used. The project research revealed that the first hurdle is peoples' varying understanding of the terminology. People tend to steer away from *conflict* and related terms or use them in strictly negative ways.

> The cornerstone assumption remains: Collaboration does not mean we all have to agree, but we do have to maintain mutual understanding.

A central premise for understanding conflict is that *conflict can be healthy and recognized as a potentially positive, energizing dynamic within the association.* The following terms related to conflict are presented in order of the fear factor associated with them.

- **Disagreement:** At least two people have different opinions on a particular issue. This does not necessarily imply a conflict or dispute and is generally resolvable.
- **Dispute:** *Black's Law Dictionary* defines a dispute as "a conflict or controversy; a conflict of claims or rights; an assertion of a right, claim, or demand on one side, met by contrary claims or allegations on the other. The subject of litigation; the matter for which a suit is brought and upon which issue is joined, and in relation to which jurors are called and witnesses are examined." Thus, a dispute is any conflict or controversy, which, if not resolved, may result in litigation. For the purpose of this manual, the term *conflict* will be used interchangeably with the term *dispute*.
- **Conflict:** A situation in which the values, conditions, practices, or goals for various participants appear to be inherently incompatible. This definition is rather static because it does not allow for relief from the conflict. According to Hawkins and Preston, writing in *Managerial Commu-*

nication, conflict is viewed as: "A struggle over values and claims to scarce status, power, and resources in which the aims of the opponents are to neutralize, injure, or eliminate their rivals."

Hawkins and Preston also state that conflict "is an interpersonal, behavioral event; it has both social characteristics and implications and is also deeply rooted in the nature of the interpersonal communication process, with an emphasis on perception." Incompatibility arising from conflict is often a function of perceived rather than actual differences.

Functional and Dysfunctional Conflict

Conflict can be productive or unproductive.

Functional, or *productive,* conflict generates productive discussion on a topic. As a result of the interaction, individuals and organizations may grow and strengthen their mission, purpose, and program.

Dysfunctional conflict (sometimes called *unproductive,* or *destructive,* conflict) may impart either a negative or positive force. This conflict can also be enduring, intense, or destructive. In this manual, the single term *conflict* will be used to denote unproductive dysfunctional conflict.

Conflict becomes a negative force in organizations when there is little or no tolerance for any type of disagreement. The intensity of a conflict that threatens to tear apart an organization or that attacks the consensual basis of a social system is proportional to the rigidity of the structure. Conflict tends to be dysfunctional or unproductive for a social structure in which there is no, or insufficient, tolerance and institutionalization of conflict.

Conflict and hostility are not the same. Rather, conflict is an outlet that allows for expression of one's hostility. Dysfunctional conflict can take on a highly personal tone, and unresolved personalized adverse issues become increasingly destructive. When this happens, a mechanism of intervention must be implemented as soon as feasible without constant interference with the normal routine or agenda—a situation that would simply create a new round of dysfunctional conflict.

Because communication theory and process are so integral to CPR, a few more terms may be helpful. The terms *dialogue, discussion,* and *consensus* refer to value systems.

- **Dialogue:** Dialogue refers to the flow of meaning. The essence of dialogue is inquiry into ideas, perceptions, and understandings. Dialogue is about exploring uncertainties and unanswered questions. The value of dialogue is in thinking together, using the combined energy of the group, and recognizing differences and enhancing collective wisdom. Associations should strive to create an environment that values and supports dialogue.

- **Discussion:** Discussions are conversations in which people speak to, address, or defend their differences.

- **Consensus:** This is a collaborative approach to group decision making. It can be a mechanism for finding out what the real issues are. Every member of the group is encouraged to present ideas and to work toward a common comfort level. Differences of opinion are not only expected but welcomed. The entire group—not the mere majority—reaches a decision through compromise and conciliation. There is no voting. This takes time but it is worth it.

ALTERNATIVE DISPUTE RESOLUTION AND COLLABORATIVE PROBLEM RESOLUTION

Facilitation is the first step in alternative dispute resolution. The CPR process, as we already have described, uses an enhanced and modified facilitation technique. An overview of the full continuum of the ADR process is outlined below for the benefit of those who may find that additional elements, such as fact-finding, negotiation, and mediation, are ultimately required.

A trained facilitator may be able to take the board through these additional steps. ADR features a continuum of processes, each of which progresses to a more formal resolution. Additionally, each process within ADR includes a progressive reliance upon facilitation or resolution by an external neutral facilitator, mediator, or arbitrator. Similar to CPR, ADR attempts to provide resolution at the basic level. (See "Comparing ADR and CPR: Two Conflict Resolution Approaches.")

Alternative dispute resolution has been adopted during the past two generations as a means to resolve conflict. Each step in the sequence must be exhausted before moving on to the next step. The process begins with communication or facilitation. The process of presenting issues may be viewed as negotiation. The parties may then progress to the next step by bringing in a neutral third party—a specialist trained in eliciting a dialogue of shared meaning to seek resolution between the parties.

As in many disciplines, ADR has its own terminology.

- *Negotiation* is the verbal give and take, or exchange, between two parties that are attempting to reach an informal or formal agreement.

COMPARING ADR AND CPR: TWO CONFLICT RESOLUTION APPROACHES

ADR (Alternative Dispute Resolution)	CPR (Collaborative Problem Resolution)
1. Generally is not implemented until problem exceeds board's capacity to resolve.	1. Features a problem or dispute generally identified early in the process.
2. Follows standard progression from negotiation to mediation to arbitration.	2. Is a more fluid process. It employs and promotes the proactive use of dialogue.
3. Is based on an adversarial relationship and approach.	3. Relies on questioning and inquiry rather than argumentation and debate.
4. Relies on a third party, such as a facilitator, mediator, or arbitrator.	4. Features a more internal communication process (dialogue).
5. Is based on a legal model.	5. Is based on a communication model.

- *Fact-finding* is a structural process in which the factual elements of a dispute are presented to a hearing officer. The process is limited to facts, and opinions are not recognized. A neutral officer reviewing the dispute makes a recommendation based on the facts provided.
- *Mediation* is a process that is led by an impartial third party. The mediator or intervener assists two parties to modify their respective positions until an agreement can be reached. Active involvement and continual negotiation with the assistance of the third party can promote resolution.
- *Arbitration* is used when the participants in a conflict mutually empower a third party to decide its outcome. They have concluded that they cannot resolve the conflict unassisted and that a neutral third party is needed. An arbitrator is mutually empowered to resolve the conflict by means of a written decision. Each of these conflict resolution models requires the use of CPR precluding the use of an external third party. This emphasizes the use of methods to resolve the conflict internally.

- *Litigation* refers to the process of moving the conflict through the judicial process. One entity within the association may sue, most likely in civil court.

Association CPR

Collaborative problem resolution, or CPR, shares its acronym with the life-saving procedure of cardiopulmonary resuscitation (only this CPR is characterized by self-intervention):

- *Collaborative* implies this is a group process for resolving group issues.
- *Problem* refers to a situation that restricts the flow of communication or the exchange of dialogue.
- *Resolution* is the mechanism whereby the CPR approach is used to provide effective closure based on mutual values.

Using this process, there are no winners or losers. All share equally in the resolution process as well as the benefits of effective decision making. The CPR approach described in this book has potential for restoring health to an association.

3

Collaborative Problem Resolution

All too often association leaders think they should be skilled in "the art of war," whereas the CPR process relies more heavily on the art of communication. Board conflict generally does not result in bloodshed! But emotions can run high. Conflict is expressed in feelings of fear, threat, mistrust, and hostility.

Conflict and hostility are not the same. Conflict is an outlet that allows for the expression of one's hostility. Dysfunctional conflict becomes personal. Unresolved adverse issues become increasingly destructive, and a mechanism of intervention must be implemented as soon as is feasible.

Prior to using the CPR process, the CEO, board chair, or a designated facilitator must lead the members through the steps of the model. It is best for the CEO to designate an internal facilitator, especially if he or she has or is likely to become directly involved in the dispute. It is not practical for the president or facilitator to suddenly stop the board meeting and move into the intervention process.

GENERAL INDICATORS OF A PROBLEM

Here are some general ways to tell if a problem is developing that could build into a conflict.

1. A board member becomes uncharacteristically silent, refrains from comment or participation, or otherwise appears disengaged.
2. The dialogue on an issue becomes stagnant. No new ideas are expressed.
3. Unstructured subgroups formed within the board, seemingly to take control of an issue.
4. A lack of trust is overwhelming the decision-making process.

THREE CRITICAL CONDITIONS FOR USING CPR

Unlike ADR or a traditional grievance mechanism, the CPR model is not rigidly structured, although the association board maintains control over every element of the process. The group as a whole must collectively agree to use CPR as an intervention mechanism for resolving disputes within the board. The CEO, board members, and, if applicable, staff and committee chairs must agree to three critical conditions:

1. Conflict is a functional component of the decision-making process. Functional conflict can be productive and dysfunctional conflict can be destructive.
2. The entire board of directors must agree on the value of a conflict resolution process, and all board members must become stakeholders in it.
3. The process is followed in sequential steps working toward closure on an issue. The process is not multiple choice; all steps should be followed. The group will agree on the ground rules necessary to work together on the process.

---

5. Disagreements on an issue turn from dialogue to filibustering in an attempt to prevent a decision being made.
6. Members become fixed in their positions to the point of nonmovement on an issue.
7. Peripheral problems are presented merely as a means to cloud the issue at hand and make decision making more difficult.

These developments burn time, which causes anger when participants come to realize they are not moving forward.

APPLYING THE CPR MODEL

The first step in intervention is determining when an issue has become dysfunctional. In many cases, conflict is not readily apparent to all other participants. Yet, covert conflict can be extremely volatile.

Conflict within any association is a natural consequence of the diversity of views and agendas within groups, and the CPR Model is predicated on the belief that a degree of conflict within an organization is healthy because it facilitates growth and creativity. It is only when conflict becomes seemingly unmanageable or destructive to an organization that a conflict resolution mechanism becomes necessary to bring order to the decision-making process. At this juncture, the CPR Model, or some other conflict resolution modality, should be implemented.

Experience has taught us that relying on the board in its entirety to determine when an organization is experiencing negative conflict, and when it should apply conflict resolution methods, is simply impracticable. This is why it is essential at the outset for any organization addressing a particular conflict to:

1. Adopt a conflict resolution process.
2. Agree on ground rules.
3. Determine who within the organization could and should be the facilitator.
4. Set guidelines to determine when conflict needs to be recognized and resolved.

Building a Conflict Resolution Process

As association leaders, we are masterful in defining how to manage day to day operations, increase membership, elect officers, and prepare board agendas. However, we commonly refuse to face the fact that people don't always agree and conflict will arise.

Whatever method will be used to resolve conflict needs to be agreed on in advance. That method should take the form of a plan that is both a part of the association's policies and procedures or operational manual and a product that is formally approved by the board of directors. It should include:

- When to use the conflict resolution procedure (e.g., at a separate meeting of the board or as part of a designated board initiative before or after the meeting).
- How the facilitator is to interact with the CEO and the board chair.
- What recourse there will be if none of the CPR or other methods to address conflict has been effective.

Under what circumstances an external facilitator is needed to facilitate the group or serve as a mediator.

INDICATORS FOR INTERVENTION

It is impossible to list all the situations in which a conflict resolution plan should be implemented. However some of the more critical indicators that arise in any organization can be identified:

Long-term conflict. Often, a problem within an organization persists over a considerable period of time to the detriment of an organization.

Recycled or repetitive problems. Although a problem may not be ongoing, it is not uncommon for a particular problem within an organization to reoccur, or revisit an organization on a periodic basis without resolution.

Personal attacks. It may be apparent that a conflict resolution plan is necessary when the board members or individual members engage in personal attacks on each other.

Intensity of meetings. While passionate discourse can be healthy under the appropriate circumstances, continuous intensity in board meetings can sometimes be not only unproductive but also destructive.

Deadlock. When it is obvious that the organization has reached an impasse on an important issue, conflict resolution may be necessary.

Disengagement. One of the most subtle indicators of a troubled board is the disengagement, or gradual withdrawal of participation, of a board member or a subgroup of the board.

Personal agendas. It is unrealistic to expect board members to leave their personal agendas outside board meetings. However, when personal agendas of certain board members begin to dominate meetings, intervention is needed.

Admittedly, the application of these indicators involves a certain degree of subjectivity by the facilitator. An unbiased facilitator may not be able to recognize negative conflict initially but will at least recognize there is some significant problem that merits exploring.

ESTABLISHING GROUND RULES

It is impractical to set forth the ground rules that should be applied to any specific organization to resolve conflict. However, some general parameters apply to any organization in addressing conflict resolution issues.

Before establishing ground rules, the group should adopt a primary principle: The organization and its board members must be fully committed to resolving negative conflicts.

The participants should draft their own ground rules to ensure ownership. The sentences—somewhere between 2 and 10—should include the words *respect, agree to disagree, no bad ideas, teamwork,* and *consensus.*

THE ROLE OF THE FACILITATOR

An Overview of Facilitation

As indicated, the conflict resolution plan adopted by an organization should describe a specific method for its selection of an individual or body within the organization who can determine if the organization is experiencing negative conflict that requires activation of the plan. How this decision is made will vary among organizations.

Facilitation has received widespread acceptance in meetings where decision making is critical. Research into the makeup of boards has shown that diversity can create the dialogue necessary to produce viable decisions. However, this same diversity of backgrounds and personalities can generate conflict. A trained facilitator's ability to meld diversity of expertise into a successful team effort is also crucial to a successful CPR process.

One caveat: Whereas elements of ADR progress from facilitation through mediation, the CPR process focuses only on facilitation. If negotiation or mediation is required, the internal facilitator should be used only if he or she also has had training in mediation.

Types of Involvement

A facilitator may have multiple functions. The facilitator may be engaged only when a conflict arises or throughout a range of board activities. Ideally, because this individual has the skills in communication and conflict resolution, those skills should be used to prevent conflict situations.

The facilitator should be involved in each of the following association activities:

Board training. The facilitator should have a central role in the annual board training, leading a review of the CPR process, the conflict ground rules, and other communication principles. Chapter 5 discusses a few key tenets of good communication and offers a board self-audit to aid in checking the health of the group.

Meeting facilitation. Because productive meetings are a primary objective, it is logical to use the facilitator to assist in the flow of other meetings, especially board meetings, not just when a conflict arises. As shown later in this chapter, step 1 of CPR is to admit that a conflict exists. Disagreements arise almost anytime individuals are asked to make a collective decision. The facilitator can assist the group in recognizing that it has a conflict and that, "We need to stop a minute and assess what is happening." A brief time out can help the board regain equilibrium.

In a nonconflict situation, the facilitator can:

- help ensure an effective, goal-oriented flow of communication
- concentrate on the structure of the interaction, allowing the participants to address the content and reach an acceptable outcome more rapidly
- promote a team effort to ensure participation from all members of the team
- neutralize attempts to dominate by one or two individuals
- assist the group in staying with the assigned agenda and guard against the adverse impact of personal agendas

Conflict resolution. Even in the most congenial board and within the most well-organized meeting, conflict can still erupt. The facilitator must be prepared to recognize the indicators and make the determination that the board or committee should put aside the agenda and resolve whatever conflict has stymied the decision making. A list of some indicators for intervention appeared earlier in this chapter.

Choosing and Training an Internal Facilitator

Training in communication and the ADR process are critical. In choosing the individual to function as facilitator, the board should recognize that he or she must:

- remain neutral
- demonstrate excellent communication skills
- be familiar with association policies and strategic plans
- be able to set aside his or her personal agenda
- remain calm during conflict resolution situations
- have the respect of the leadership

It is essential to the process to select a facilitator who will be in a position to objectively evaluate the organization's ability to deal with conflict and to fairly apply the conflict resolution plan when deemed necessary. Here are some other criteria.

1. The facilitator must be as unbiased, neutral, and objective as reasonably possible. A facilitator who is motivated in large part by his or her per-

sonal agenda will not be as inclined to invoke the conflict resolution process based on actual indications of negative conflict.

2. The facilitator should be an individual who is not directly subordinate to, or under the influence of, the CEO, chairman, or other authority within the organization. (This is difficult to achieve unless someone is hired to do it.)

3. The facilitator should have at least some experience in dealing with conflict.

Lastly, the individual should be able to make a commitment of at least two years to the position of facilitator, particularly if training is necessary. Someone with knowledge of communication and the ADR process easily understands the CPR process and may not require additional training. However, an individual with no formal education or experience will need to become knowledgeable about both disciplines and will find that a number of good communication and ADR training programs are available.

CRITICAL ELEMENTS OF CPR

CPR is a five-step process. As shown in the chart in the preceding chapter, which compared alternative dispute resolution and communication models, CPR incorporates elements of both ADR and effective communication.

It is critical to note that the five steps of CPR are sequential, and the process requires completing each step before moving on to the next step. These steps help to break the conflict into its logical parts and resolve it by moving from accepting that there is a problem to setting the goals for closure. The process focuses on the nature and cause of the actual conflict, identifies the primary players, frames the problem so that it can be resolved, and finally synthesizes or summarizes the outcome or resolution of the conflict.

Now let us look at the five steps. They are:

1. Accept and activate awareness
2. Aim
3. Acknowledge
4. Seek accountability and address
5. Award

Step 1. Accept and activate awareness.

The most difficult step is initiating the process—when the facilitator has determined that a conflict has become unmanageable and a particular issue requires that another mechanism be used. As emphasized throughout this book, this is not to be construed as a failure on the part of the CEO, board, or leadership. The crux of the problem is that boards often avoid step 1. The board is accepting responsibility, not accusing. By acknowledging that the board is experiencing conflict, the board has taken that first step.

It is crucial that the group recognizes the need to use a process that will resolve the conflict. The natural reaction is to blame, flee, or try to fight the problem, which is counterproductive. Taking this first step may be a struggle for the group, but after it has been utilized once or twice, it will become very natural and the group will easily become aware of how well it is functioning.

This aspect of step 1 requires that the board see the need and value in shifting its mindset from its agenda items to the process through which it can accomplish its objectives.

Here is how to use step 1:

1. The facilitator moves the group from the formal agenda to communication process whose purpose is to resolve a conflict that has arisen.
2. Without placing blame or fault, the group identifies the destructive conflict generators and accepts the need for managing the conflict.
3. Together, the group reviews the ground rules that activate the process.

Step 2. Aim.

The participants must ask, What do we want? How do we get what we want? The questioning does not include why, since this question simply encourages placing blame. The aim is the goal or purpose of the process. It will be achieved when the group reaches closure on the issue about which there is conflict.

Step 3. Acknowledge.

This step seeks the pivotal issues. What is the true nature of the conflict? To address the real issue, the stakeholders must identify the core issue. This is a brainstorming process and not merely an opportunity to vent. Therefore, it has to be carefully managed. The group must know that this exercise needs a time limit and understand that its focus is on identifying related issues.

Once a workable list is developed (most likely on a flipchart), the group can eliminate items that are beyond the scope of the board discussion, such that the remaining items are those that can be expected to be resolved along with the pivotal issue. The group then places a priority on the pivotal issues and determines whether any of them can be addressed at a later date. This activity may appear time-consuming but will save time in the long run. Time ultimately may be allocated to discuss emotional issues that contributed to or are a part of the issue. In many situations, listing the issues may actually move the board to closure and settle the conflict.

How to use step 3:

1. The facilitator draws out concerns and issues from the participants and lists the items on a flipchart. Allow about 30 minutes for this activity.
2. The group evaluates the list to make sure it includes the issue that originally caused the group to use the CPR process. If not, are the issues listed more or less important than the original issue? If only one issue is listed, it must be recognized as the primary concern.
3. Strike issues from the list that cannot be resolved because of their nature or the fact they are irrelevant to the core conflict. (Those issues stricken from the list can be held for later consideration.)

Step 4. Seek accountability and address.

At this point, the facilitator asks, "What do you want and who do you think is accountable for getting you there?" Who is affected by the problem? Who should be involved in the process? At this juncture the stakeholders may determine who has to provide additional information. What, if any, outside groups or committees are being affected and may be incorporated into the process?

After these questions have been addressed so that the group has achieved some degree of comfort, it may collectively agree to assign the pivotal issue to a subgroup, to analyze the issue and present alternative solutions. The stakeholders may experience anxiety or become uncomfortable with the recognition of all the secondary stakeholders affected by the conflict and the additional participants required to resolve the issue.

This is the group's opportunity to frame and reframe the issue. First, take the primary issue and figuratively place the problem inside a glass cube.

Think of this step as the opportunity to look at the issue from different perspectives.

Another way of addressing the reasons and roots of the issue is to mentally place it on a stage, visualizing the issue from the balcony, then from the front row, and then from backstage.

The group will readily conclude that every conflict is multifaceted and can be seen from more than one side. The glass cube serves as a shield for personal attacks and emotional outbursts. Remember that this is a linear but not a rigidly structured process; rather, it is an opportunity to engage in directed dialogue. Reframing helps to restate the issue using positive language while, at the same time, explaining the problem.

Moreover, the act of reframing allows the stakeholders to understand anew the adage, "crisis means opportunity." One person may see a situation as a crisis but framing the issue with a new perspective provides the opportunity to view the issue—or fellow participants—in another light (e.g., an individual may be seen as "a raving lunatic disruptive to the agenda," or, reframed, "as an enthusiastic person excited about new ideas"). The goal is for participants to discover new perspectives in viewing a problem.

How to use step 4:

1. Write the issue in precise language on a flipchart. Be creative! What do you know about the issue? How does it look from different perspectives? What do you see that you did not see before?
2. Now, restate the issue using only positive descriptors. If there are two points of view, state both in positive language.
3. Address what needs to be done to achieve resolution.
4. Identify the modifications as well as the resources that may be necessary to do so.

Step 5. Award.

The goal of all the steps is ultimately to reach closure. Closure is acknowledged when the aim is achieved. Can a concluding statement or report be provided to the stakeholders? If a subgroup recommended a resolution, do the stakeholders as a whole endorse that recommendation for resolution?

Finally, state the issue in the form of an amendment. It is imperative that all participants agree on closure and that a written document, statement, or report recording that agreement is available for future review. The document can

C.P.R. MODEL

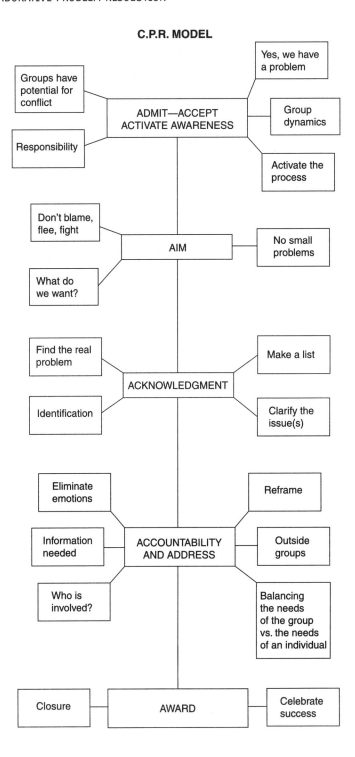

include the assignments to certain individuals or subgroups for preparation for the next meeting. However, it must *not* place blame. It has to be positive in tone.

Last Thoughts

The research, survey results, and communication tips have a lot to say about useful preventive measures. These five steps can be effective in resolving conflicts of varying sources and degrees of contentiousness. In the event that the board is unsuccessful in coming to closure on the dispute, an external mediator may have to be engaged.

Another point to keep in mind is that although CPR can be effective in providing resolution through dialogue, the model is not guaranteed to resolve all disputes. (The adversarial ADR continuum may be required.) CPR is a convenient acronym when thinking of a process to breathe new life into your association. But it is most important to focus on prevention first.

4

Causes and Consequences of Conflict

IDENTIFYING SOURCES OF CONFLICT

The research and personal interviews conducted by the ASAE Foundation helped to formulate a list of sources that can cause conflict. Reviewing the sources that may generate conflict and quite possibly exacerbate a dispute within the board is a valuable prevention tool. Some of these sources of conflict are unavoidable merely because of the nature of volunteer interactions.

By no means should the list be used to place blame on any individual or individuals. It merely serves to sensitize leadership to possible sources of conflict. A periodic review by the association leadership to identify ways of reducing the impact of these common situations is another valuable tool. Let's look at 10 of these potential causes of conflict.

1. Personal agendas. A board member may have ulterior motives for serving on the board. Human nature dictates that many, if not all, of the board members carry into the boardroom personal and professional agendas that may be contrary to the fundamental purpose of the association or the group agenda.

2. Power brokers. When an overbearing board member dominates the meeting or attempts to change the course of the agenda, conflict is predictable. Power brokers often achieve their position because of real or perceived seniority. These individuals may instigate a turf battle and use it to execute their own agenda. Self-designated power brokers attempting to impose a personal agenda can also generate conflict.

3. Lack of unity and organization. An association without a current strategic plan, mission statement, goals and objectives, and shared vision faces multiple sources of conflict. Board members need a collective purpose; absent that, individual board members naturally impose their personal interpretation on an amorphous plan. This can undermine the foundation of the association.

4. Subgroup subversion. A few board members may have developed agendas within a subgroup that differ dramatically from the actual mission statement of the association. A diversion may occur as a ploy to replace the executive director or to change another leadership position.

5. Resistance to change. Change is difficult and transition periods can be extremely painful. When the CEO, the board, or selected members refuse to accept change that is necessary for the growth of the association, dysfunctional conflict is the inevitable result. Uncontrolled growth causes conflict similar to the transitions that change brings about. The association's particular profession, trade, or cause may be experiencing rapid growth but the association is not prepared or willing to address current needs.

6. Chief executive officer and the job description. The research conducted for this project indicates that some CEOs are working without a job description approved by the board. Further, the research has identified the fact that some CEOs may not be in full agreement with the parameters of their job description. Certain members of the association or board may have different perceptions of the job or recognize that changes to their role need to be made to sustain the viability of the association.

7. Lack of structure. Conflict can surface when a board is not functioning within a defined process or policies and procedures. Survey responses indicated a strong desire for a well-organized meeting and active agenda for the members to address.

8. Stagnant staff. When staff members are not motivated, not communicating, and not recognizing (or fulfilling) their particular roles and functions, conflict can also occur. One staff member can generate a significant conflict and negatively affect the operation of the board. Open lines of communication between the board and executive staff must be maintained or conflict can surface.

9. Withdrawal. One of the most consistent findings in the surveys and interviews was the seeming compulsion of association boards to handle conflict by walking away from it or acting as if it is just not there. Association executives and board members apparently tend to withdraw from conflict because they perceive it as failure. However, board members may find it easiest to withdraw from the individual instigating the conflict, which only serves to alienate that person further. It generally does not resolve the issues.

10. **Lack of diversity.** Boards ideally seek members who offer differing points of view, diverse backgrounds and expertise, and different personalities and interests. As a result, conflict is inherent with this valuable abundance of diversity. If the association's board does not have diversity of backgrounds, expertise, or personalities, it is facing an even bigger problem: the lack of qualified decision making and representation.

CONSEQUENCES OF CONFLICT

The result of conflict could be strengthening of the association mission, increased services to the membership, a revitalized vision, or more effective leadership. This, of course, occurs when conflict can be resolved or channeled into productive activity. Anyone who has ever become enmeshed in conflict between members of a board of an association and the CEO, for example, knows all too well that conflict is more likely to destroy than to strengthen if it is allowed to escalate.

Conflict, whether it is directed toward specific issues, is a manifestation of a chronic disparity of vision, or is a function of generational or technological communication barriers, can have permanent and fatal consequences. Disputes between board members and association executives are damaging and can result in the alienation of the executive or board member if it is enduring and exceptionally contentious.

The association CEO may expend valuable time, money, and energy addressing unresolved conflicts, regardless of the size of the association or the extent of the dispute. Because irate members seldom view any problem as insignificant, any conflict can absorb large amounts of staff time and resources. Discussed below are several consequences of conflict, many of which the seasoned board member or CEO director will relate to immediately. The least of the conflicts would be enduring unhappiness or discontent among the board members.

- Conflict can be all consuming for the CEO and can redirect energy from productive activities to reactionary management.
- Board members may elect to "disengage" or become apathetic. Disengaging refers to members who show their discontent or disapproval by withdrawing. Periodic silence or refraining from involvement on a particular issue does not indicate a member's disengagement, although body lan-

guage or actions counter to the member's normal level of participation may. When there is genuine disengagement, the board may be losing a valuable asset. Rather than face or become embroiled in a conflict, the board member may even resign from the board or the association.

- The board may determine that the source of conflict rests solely with the CEO or a staff member and may conclude that the problem will disappear if that individual is removed. If, in fact, this is a major source of conflict and no resolution is possible, then such an action may be appropriate.

- Participation in board meetings, on committees, and in other leadership activities may decline. Although at times it seems that some board members relish the fighting and contention, others may decide to drop out of leadership participation altogether.

- Membership, especially in a small association, is sensitive to the environment within the leadership of the association. Large associations, or associations with active competitors, are equally vulnerable. Serious or enduring conflict can easily result in loss of membership.

- There have been too many instances in which conflict has been so divisive that associations have split into separate entities. However, when members are in conflict over the mission or values, this action may be seen as the only solution.

- One of the most serious consequences of conflict, or the concluding phase of a conflict, may be litigation.

- The CEO or staff may decide that the conflict "isn't worth it" and resign. An event of this magnitude can seriously disrupt the association.

Obviously, litigation of an uncontrolled dispute is not on any association's *things I want to do* list. We are living in a litigious world where bringing suit sometimes seems to be the only alternative. But going to court can be a horrendous expense without necessarily providing a workable resolution.

The collaborative problem resolution process has a similar mission to the ADR process. The goal is to resolve disputes and ultimately to prevent a costly and time-consuming court battle. Discussions with association executives and a review of court dockets reveal that associations are finding themselves in court on issues that initially appeared trivial or petty but escalated, crushing budgets and strangling membership.

The phrase *day-in-court* has significant meaning in the CPR process. Many people invest the time, energy, and money to sue just to be heard. The

CPR process affords the disgruntled member the opportunity to be heard and, more important, the opportunity to become involved in resolving the issue. The board and CEO should not address a problem only for the purpose of staying out of court, but they need to understand that the ultimate outcome may be litigation.

WHAT SHOULD BE THE ROLE OF AN ATTORNEY ON THE BOARD?

A discussion of the role of an attorney to the board is appropriate. Boards all too often assume that appointing an attorney to the board will either help avoid conflict or offer an easy means of resolution. However, the attorney should not be considered the legal counsel for the board.

Many board members inappropriately consider having an attorney attend meetings of the board of directors to be a prudent, cost-saving measure for free legal advice. A legal mind is always valuable to any board for advice on incorporation, business, securities, and drafting bylaws.

Clearly, the mere attendance and participation of an attorney with a board of directors will not necessarily facilitate the resolution of disputes, nor will an attorney's involvement at a board meeting prevent serious conflict or even ultimate litigation. In fact, oftentimes attorneys may, because of their particular training and perspective, be more focused on an adversarial than an amicable resolution short of litigation.

On the plus side, however, the perspective of an attorney with an association board may be beneficial in assessing the particular merits as well as the issues involved in a dispute, and in evaluating the possible outcomes of a dispute in the event of litigation—a possibility that should always be carefully considered and weighed in any dispute.

One interview subject in the foundation's research, who is an attorney and an active board member, offers this perspective on the propriety of attorneys serving on boards:

Question: As an attorney, a volunteer, and the recognized legal counsel on the board, do you find that other board members gravitate to you to resolve disputes?

Answer: "That can happen. But you need to make clear what your role is and be sure everyone understands it. I have been on boards as a board member, and when legal issues come up, people have turned to me and said, 'OK, what do we do? How do we resolve this?' And I said, 'Well, I can tell you generally, but I'm not going to give you legal advice about this issue because I can't as a board member. If you want me to be your legal advisor, then you need to fire me from the board and you need to have me be your lawyer only.' And that's really another pretty common area of conflict, because people always want to have lawyers on their boards and don't realize that they can't give them legal advice properly within the ethics rules. They need to do one or the other."

Question: Have you ever seen disputes that can be short term—where the board just gets in there and handles it—or have you ever been on a board that just has lingering long-term disputes that don't seem to get resolved?

Answer: "Yes, to both. And one occasion has turned into litigation. It shouldn't have been a long-term dispute, but it turned out that way."

Members of a board should be mindful that an attorney on a board should not be called on to render legal opinions. Whereas he or she may be helpful in drafting bylaws and other documents as well as pointing out legal issues, the attorney can be placed in an untenable conflict-of-interest position if asked to render legal opinions, which call for a measure of objectivity. He or she may lack the requisite training or experience in a particular area and may feel compromised if he or she thinks other board members are basing their decisions in whole or in part on his or her legal acumen.

Rather than looking to the attorney board member for legal opinions, the board should seek direction and guidance from the attorney by asking him to focus on the appropriate or essential legal issues and direct the board to engage, if necessary, a legal expert in the subject area.

5

Preventive Measures

Ideally, this manual would provide the association's leadership with a silver bullet—or at least some workable process designed to avoid conflict. The fact is that as long as associations comprise members of the human race, disagreements, arguments, and conflict will occur.

As we have previously pointed out, these conflicts are all right and can even be very healthy. The challenge is to prevent the conflict from taking on a life of its own, preventing the board from carrying out the important missions and goals of the association and, most important, limiting the effectiveness of the decision-making process.

This chapter offers a collection of practical suggestions, background information, and tools that individually or collectively can help to maintain a positive, productive atmosphere for the board to transact business. Because the scene of most of the conflict either is initiated at a board meeting or becomes hostile and disruptive at a board meeting, a short discussion of planning for productive meetings is offered.

Communication is crucial to any successful transaction, negotiation, or conversation. For this reason, we offer a number of techniques and considerations to strengthen communication between board members, other association members, the CEO, and staff.

MEETING DYNAMICS

Adopting a structured process for board meetings is a crucial element in preventing unproductive conflict, but its success depends on the total involvement of all the participants in all the steps. If a board has a history of becoming disjointed, the chair or president may have a designated facilitator to coach the group through the essential steps of the meeting process.

It is important to stipulate that neither the CEO nor board chair can lead the meeting and serve as facilitator. The facilitator does not preside over the meeting nor interrupt the person directing the meeting but rather assists with the process. The five steps may appear cumbersome at first, but these, too, will become routine with repetition.

Step 1. Pre-meeting preparation. Preliminary meeting arrangements are essential. The facilitator should secure a meeting room that is convenient, comfortable, and controllable, with a minimum of distractions, such as discomfort caused by poor climate control in the room.

Ensuring that the room is comfortable and well equipped may appear basic to some readers. Yet this attention to detail sends the message that the leadership understands the board's time constraints. Have all participants been properly contacted and are any specially invited guests required for specific input on a particular issue? The facilitator should coordinate with the association's meeting planner to ensure that certain materials will reach participants prior to the meeting, including the agenda and supporting documents. Valuable time is saved when board members have everything they need at hand to immediately address agenda items.

2. Preparing and prioritizing. A properly sequenced agenda with items prioritized is absolutely critical. Each agenda item should have an allotted period of time for presentation, discussion and, if required, voting. Each item on the agenda should be identified as an information, action, or discussion item. To the best of their ability, the meeting chair, CEO, and facilitator should insist on maintaining the preset order of the agenda items and the length of discussion. (Some boards find it useful to use a consent agenda or to discuss items and then vote later.)

3. Performing. This is the meeting step in which the anticipation, by all involved, is that the real work will be accomplished. Tough decisions will be made, action items will be addressed that will move the association forward, and members will focus on the policy issues. More than likely, this is also the point in the meeting where personal agendas, power plays, and disagreements will escalate into full-blown disputes. Using *Robert's Rules of Order* or a similar structure is important here because the process is known and consistent—and there is general agreement that it works. Effective communication techniques and strong leadership are critical at this step of the process.

4. Product. A successful board meeting is one that is productive: The required outcome is achieved and members can see a tangible benefit from their time and effort. Not everyone is going to be happy; not everyone is going to believe that the process was appropriate or the outcomes beneficial to the association. However, if board members walk away with an overall sense of accomplishment, then the meeting will have produced the desired results.

5. Pursuit of closure. Closure is critical to the success of each board meeting. Regardless of how many action items were approved, if follow-up is neglected, conflict is inevitable. A chart listing the action item, the date it is to be initiated as well as completed, and the responsible person should be sent to each board member within a specified period after the meeting, along with the minutes or meeting summary.

The sequential steps of the actual meeting are important to the decision-making process as well as a measure to prevent dysfunctional conflict. The process described above identifies the individual steps necessary to initiate and maintain a cohesive meeting process. In addition, the following chart offers a valuable review prior to the meeting. Such a chart can be used to delegate and track completion of tasks and responsibilities and may be a useful addition to the association's new member orientation.

THE BOARD MEETING

1. Pre-meeting Preparation

- Meeting Site Room Arrangements

    Convenient

    Comfortable

    Controllable

- PRELIMINARY PHASE

- PHILOSOPHIZE—Determine outcomes desired and approach needed to achieve them.

- Is the physical environment conducive to positive interaction? (e.g., temperature, lighting, seating arrangement, microphones)

---

continued

- Have all member arrangements been fully disseminated? (e.g., travel, start time, meals, location)
- Has all material been disseminated at least 10 days before the meeting?

2. Planning and Prioritizing

- AGENDA—Items to be addressed at this meeting.
- CONCEPTUALIZING
- SETTING TIMELINES—List member concerns.
- Prioritize the discussion and action items—easy issues first if possible.
- TIME MANAGEMENT—Give each item a specified time . . . begin and come back, if needed.
- Have all members had an opportunity to provide agenda items?
- Has a board book been assembled prior to the meeting?
- Set ground rules (e.g., 3 to 5 minute responses by members unless permission is granted for longer discourse)
- Follow *Robert's Rules of Order* or other generally accepted rules.
- Determine how closely meeting protocol will be followed.

3. Performing and Producing

- PREVENT POWER PLAYS—The president must accept the responsibility to maintain a balance of power between the CEO and board members.
- Have roles and responsibilities been clearly delineated and communicated?

- Has commonality of purpose been defined and agreed on?
- Is there an opportunity for presentation of varying perspectives?
- Is the chair maintaining focus on the agenda items?
- PRESENTATION—Is there the appropriate amount of dialogue?
- Is everyone respectful of all members' positions?
- Are members sensitive to the need to avoid micromanagement issues?
- Has a summary of decisions made been given at the end of the meeting?

4. Packaging

- ACTION PLANS
- State responsible party and timeline for each approved action item.
- Provide an assignment sheet for every action item.
- Set next meeting. Identify items that did not reach closure.
- Do board minutes accurately reflect issues and decisions?
- Are board minutes free of negative references to members' positions?

5. Post-meeting Follow-up

- Have the action plans and assignment sheets been reviewed?
- Have the action items been accomplished on the time schedule that was approved?

A SELF-AUDIT FOR BOARD MEMBERS

1. What do you believe is the role of board of directors? (Prioritize the top three with 1 being the highest.)

   __Manage day-to-day business

   __Review association policy

   __Oversee association procedures

   __Direct staff activities

   __Budget development

   __Monitor expenditures

   __Ensure bylaws compliance

   __Make strategic decisions for the future of the association

2. I am serving on the board because of the opportunity to: (Check all that are relevant.)

   ☐ Change the direction of the board or association

   ☐ Maintain the direction of the board or association

   ☐ Enhance my career

   ☐ Assist in accomplishing the mission of the organization

   ☐ Represent my peers

   ☐ Increase my personal power base and networking opportunities

   ☐ Grow professionally

   ☐ Obtain promotion

   ☐ Other_____

3. Are the board members and staff communicating frequently enough?

   ☐ Yes   ☐ No

4. Are board meetings sometimes unproductive?

   ☐ Yes   ☐ No

SELF-AUDIT FOR ASSOCIATION LEADERSHIP

In this section, a short self-audit or self-assessment tool is presented. The questions included in the 10-question audit were taken from the written survey for the foundation research project. Uncertain or negative answers on these questions were indicators that the association may have discontented members.

5. If yes, list the top three reasons why you perceive they sometimes become unproductive?

   1.

   2.

   3.

6. Does your association have a mission and vision statement?

   ☐ Yes   ☐ No

7. Were your staff or board of directors instrumental in developing the mission and vision statement?

   ☐ Yes   ☐ No

8. How familiar are you with the mission and vision statement?

   ☐ Totally

   ☐ Not totally

   ☐ Somewhat

   ☐ Less than somewhat

   ☐ Not at all

9. How comfortable are you in recommending change to the board?

   ☐ Completely comfortable

   ☐ Very comfortable

   ☐ Comfortable

   ☐ Less than comfortable

   ☐ Not at all

Please explain: _____

10. Do you understand your role as a member of the board of directors?

    ☐ Yes   ☐ No   ☐ Somewhat

One consistent concern centered around the formulation or understanding of the association's mission and goals statements. If there is ambiguity between mission and practice or between goals and association activities, the members indicated a sense of discontinuity. Similarly, defined roles for board members, the CEO, and staff are important in maintaining effective management and leadership. (See Appendix A and Appendix B)

The self-audit can be used as a board orientation tool or as a mechanism to be occasionally employed by the CEO or board chair. The questionnaire should be completed in confidence and no identifiers used on the form (that is, coding or other mechanisms for identifying the individual completing the survey). People are more likely to provide candid responses if there is no fear of identification. The responses are merely guides for the leadership to identify areas of concern among members.

For example, if a number of members indicate that board meetings are frequently or even occasionally unproductive, the association's leadership needs to review the meeting process to improve timeliness and productivity. Identifying appropriate roles and carrying out those roles is critical to sound association management. The audit or assessment can identify whether there is confusion regarding roles. Given the critical role of good communication, any indication of a breakdown in communication should be immediately addressed.

COMMUNICATION AND CONFLICT

A friend once reminded me of the adage; "It is easy for the preacher to preach to the choir." When conflict surfaces, effective communication becomes even more critical. Obviously, it takes effective communication strategies to ensure that conflict is a functional and productive tool. The communicators, for example, the board chair, must be cognizant of the perceptions that he or she and the other members bring to the table. They must listen to both dialogue and body language as well as provide feedback. These three elements of the communication process are discussed in greater detail later in this chapter.

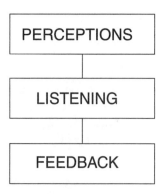

A few years ago I watched Lee Trevino accept the championship at a major golf tournament on the seniors tour. In his interview afterward, the seasoned professional credited his win to spending time on the range with his pro working on a few basics. I was impressed that a highly successful golf professional took time to review his grip, backswing, and follow-through. I relate this story to association professionals, because in communication, one's review of the most basic skills can be essential. Skills are honed for the conflict tournament.

PERCEPTIONS

I recall an amusing—and true—attempt at resolving an issue between an association and a government agency. As the situation unfolded, it became a classic example of a "problem with perceptions." During a semiannual river running trek, I would always include a visit to an elderly homesteader in Central Utah. Pearl, a feisty octogenarian, was an author, teacher, ranch-hand, and the first female president of the Eastern Utah Cattleman's Association.

On one of my visits, she asked if I would deliver a letter to the State Office of Natural Resources concerning a land-use dispute with a federal agency. I asked about the local cattle ranchers' dispute over grazing rights. The cattleman's association planned a special meeting to resolve the dispute.

Indeed, the ranchers and the government agency convened a meeting, but not a word was exchanged. I asked Pearl why. "Well," exclaimed Pearl, "the government sent us a young woman from California with absolutely no ranching experience!"

"How did you find this out?" I inquired. "Well, she was too young to know about land-use disputes. She had a sunburn, so she was obviously from California. Most of all, showing up in that dress, she proved she had never been on a ranch!" In actual fact, the representative was the daughter of a rancher. She had just returned from a two-day cattle drive, thus the sunburn. The dispute continues.

Perceptions are culturally generated. They also are influenced by environment, social structure, age, experience, and biases. Perceptions become a personal filter to judge and ascertain intent, personal reality, and fact. They are heavily influenced by patterns of communication.

The story of Pearl is true. The federal representative's attire, age, and gender influenced the message and interrupted the flow of the communication process. Pearl, a woman with many decades of ranching experience, still cannot accept the notion of a "woman rancher." At least not a young one!

Recognize that all board members have a stake in the meeting and in the outcome.

Following are three hints for dealing with perceptions:

1. Discuss perceptions of previous meetings.
2. Think about what you would do in the other person's situation.
3. Review your fears, and regularly raise your level of awareness to the fact that your fears are based on your perceptions.

LISTENING

In some eastern cultures, it is the responsibility of the listener to understand what the speaker is communicating. Western culture tells us that it is the speaker's responsibility to ensure that the listener receives the message. Perhaps it is really a partnership and the responsibility should be shared!

A board meeting is an ideal arena for enhancing our skills. The time is restricted, the agenda is full, and little attention can be given to each separate agenda item. Listed below are some barriers to active listening along with some remedies.

1. Assumptions. As the above comments on perceptions suggest, it's a bad idea to judge another person (a speaker, a board member) too soon. Appearances, mannerisms, or biases should not become a barrier to active listening. Ask yourself what this speaker can offer to increase your knowledge or assist the board in making a decision.

2. Domination of the discussion. Communicating is a joint venture. If you find yourself dominating the conversation during the meeting, you are losing the opportunity to listen. A barrier occurs when a participant is overanxious to interject a position rather than allowing the speaker to clarify his or her position.

3. Faking attention. Don't fake attention by pretending to listen to the other board members. Figure out what is causing you to be distracted or blocked so you can again turn your full attention to listening. Attention can be diverted by small noises outside the room or preoccupation with another activity, job assignment, or demanding family situation. Make a note to remind yourself to address the situation at another time. Be present and focus your attention on the now.

4. Getting bogged down in facts. Listen for all the facts and the ideas behind the facts. A presenter may give seven facts about a particular issue and the listener will get bogged down on the first fact by trying to apply it to the problem. Or another fact may hit an emotional or personal bias, mentally blocking the listener from hearing the remaining facts. Thus, selective listening fragments the list of facts and the listener becomes disinterested because the facts become illogical.

5. Word biases. Everyone has biases against certain words and expressions. A personal experience may build a prejudice against a common term. Derogatory and defamatory terms stifle one's ability to listen. Certain overused terms, cliches, or other expressions prevent active listening, causing listeners to work even harder at gaining understanding—or to simply give up.

6. Nonverbal distractions. Nonverbal communication solicits or restricts listening depending on how the speaker uses body language. People also "listen" with their eyes by watching nonverbal cues. This becomes an automatic part of the process over one's lifetime. A speaker can encourage active listening by using changing facial expressions and hand gestures as well as by making eye contact.

FEEDBACK

Communication is a circular process: Active communication requires feedback from the listener. Generally, the feedback takes the form of a spoken response, but it may also become evident through nonverbal cues such as facial expressions, body positioning, and gesturing.

For example, board meetings conducted using *Robert's Rules of Order* have feedback built into the formal process. However, a formal process does not ensure adequate feedback. A "call for questions" or a "call for vote" may be met with a simple yea or nay or even silence. A chair or facilitator should encourage feedback without allowing lengthy or tangential, or inappropriate discussion. This is not a skill that comes naturally to many people.

Feedback is an instrument panel to gauge the degree of understanding achieved through the communication process. Giving feedback represents the listener's effort to arrive at the speaker's intended meaning or understanding, and that completes the communication circle.

FORMS OF FEEDBACK

There are many ways to enhance feedback in the negotiating environment. Here are some suggestions.

1. **Ask questions.** You can go directly to the other person(s) and ask questions that verify or refute your understanding. This helps ensure that perceptions have not created a misunderstanding or miscommunication.

2. **Watch facial expressions and reactions.** Be vigilant for reactions from the receiver that may indicate that your communication is not being understood as you intended.

3. **Have the other person repeat the message.** Alternatively, you can repeat the message and gain confirmation that it is understood. By having the person you are communicating with repeat the message, you can determine if he or she understands. Also, you can restate the message differently to underscore its meaning.

4. **Create and maintain a climate that encourages feedback.** One of the best ways to ensure understanding is to create a climate that encourages people to seek and receive feedback. When an individual's statements are challenged or hostility permeates the meeting, feedback is then—perhaps unintentionally—discouraged.

5. **Accept that feedback must be offered and received as part of the communication process.** The more intense or strained the situation is, the more important feedback becomes. It may be important to reiterate comments or statements made by board members.

6. **Close by summarizing key decision points. Confirm with members that your synthesis was accurate.** If it wasn't, ask for their input to modify it.

7. **Consider "lighten up" ideas to enhance the flow of communication and to direct focus to the communication process.** A few examples: Reward input or good ideas with cheap toys. (It works.) Watch for cartoons that express a specific point. Show the old Abbott and Costello film clip, "Who's on First?" for a 10-minute humorous example of communicating without getting anywhere.

Appendix A
Leadership Checklist for the Board Chair

Your leadership is critical to a healthy association. Periodically review this checklist to make sure you maintain focus on the most critical elements.

- Does your association have a vision statement, a mission statement, and goals that correspond to them?
- Do the CEO, board chair, and executive committee agree on the priority or tasks required of the CEO?
- Is the board knowledgeable, in agreement with, and conversant about the association's vision?
- Are you leading with the vision in mind?
- As board chair, are you prepared to effect the changes needed to meet the needs of your organization?
- Have you met with the CEO to prepare a smooth transition of leadership?
- Are your expectations of the board and the association during your tenure achievable?
- Does your communication style invite participation and support?
- Are conflict-of-interest statements required for all board members? If such a statement is required of one, it should be required of all.
- Are you "celebrating success" within your organization? Do you have a plan to applaud yourself, individual board members, and the organization as a whole?

Appendix B
Leadership Checklist for the CEO

Your leadership is critical to a healthy association. Periodically review this checklist to make sure you maintain focus on the most critical elements.

- Do you differentiate your managerial tasks and leadership roles as CEO? (managerial, daily administration, leadership, long-term planning)
- Does your organization have a written long-term vision, workable mission statement, and goals that correspond to them?
- Are you guided by this long-term vision as you lead your association?
- Is the board comfortable with the vision statement, and has it accepted ownership of its content?
- Do you have an effective plan to accommodate a smooth transition of volunteer leadership?
- Does the association staff have an internal conflict resolution plan, as opposed to looking to the board to resolve differences?
- Does your communication style invite participation and support?
- Are your expectations of the board and board chair explicit and focused? Are the expectations achievable?
- Have you conveyed your support to the board chair and your willingness to support the effectiveness of the board?
- Do you have a plan to continuously "celebrate success" within your organization? (This guide is for resolving problems and addressing difficult issues. How are you individually and collectively applauding the resolution of problems and issues?)

Appendix C
Case Study: The Equine Training and Taming Association

Note: This is the first of two case studies derived from the research conducted for this book. In both studies, the association and participants' names are completely fictitious.

BACKGROUND

The Equine Training and Taming Association is a ninety-year-old professional organization straddling the United States and Canada. ETTA (as affectionately nicknamed by its members) comprises professionals specifically skilled in taming wild horses and training horses to compete in riding activities. Thirty percent of the membership income is derived from equine training.

It is divided into five regions. The Western Region, which has the largest membership, covers Utah, Idaho, Montana, Wyoming, and California. In the Western Region, most members maintain a single ranch as sole practitioners with family assistance. Three members own ranches in two states. Another member, Mark, owns a multistate operation with ranches in three states and a combined staff of 85 trainers and laborers.

The ETTA board of directors consists of eight members plus the CEO and the board chair, totaling 10 voting members. The ETTA office is located in Boise, Idaho, but the CEO attempts to hold board meetings in various locations, rotating states to minimize travel and limit members' time away from their responsibilities.

ETTA provides its members with:

- updated information on equine equipment, supplies, feeds, and medical components

- legislative-municipal watches for government intervention on horse-breaking issues
- annual horse auctions (for members only)
- group purchase power on equine medicine and specialty grains
- preservation of the profession

All these products and services are important, but the group buying power (for grains and medical supplies) is what makes the membership particularly valuable.

SUMMARY OF THE PROBLEM

The CEO, Paul, and the new board chair, Peter, encountered this situation:

Board meetings have been consumed with tension and dysfunctional conflict. In fact, two newly elected members have considered resigning from the board after attending their first meeting. Naturally, as in most dysfunctional conflict situations, blame has been targeted toward the CEO and board chair. As a new board chair, Peter had the foresight to read the book on collaborative problem resolution and decides to nip the problem in the bud.

IMPLEMENTING CPR

Reviewing this situation, Peter and Paul determined it was necessary to implement a collaborative problem resolution program. This case study is written from the perspective of Peter, the board chair, and shows how he walked ETTA through CPR:

The first thing I did was ask Paul to draft a letter to board members acknowledging first that he recognized that the board members' time is valuable, but then recommending that the board convene two hours before the regularly scheduled meeting.

Paul's letter explained that this two-hour block was designated to assess the operation of the board and address issues that negatively affect the board meetings as well as the board's decision-making process—basically to restore the peace and maximize effectiveness. Between ourselves, we compared the board meeting agenda to going on a vacation by car, because first it's necessary to tune up the auto. "We can't drive and fix at the same time."

Paul proposed the entire board write mutually agreeable guidelines to clarify our purpose and ensure our time would be spent efficiently. We came up with the following ground rules, wrote them on a large flipchart, and posted them on the wall to serve as a looming reminder throughout the meeting:

- All board members are involved.
- We must maintain a dialogue (not merely a discussion, but an exchange of ideas) with the intent of resolving our efficiency issues.
- We will demonstrate respect for each other in this and future meetings. We agree that we will disagree and understand that such differences will always exist and should be used to benefit the group.
- This meeting will focus solely on developing a program to achieve more effective board meetings. We intend to avoid including items that are appropriate for—and intended to be handled in—the regularly scheduled board meeting.
- We agree to implement the problem resolution program that Peter recently learned in a seminar. (*Why not? None of us have any ideas on how to approach this issue.*)
- The purpose of the meeting is to seek resolution, not to place blame.

With the preliminary setting, our board's first step in the CPR process was to admit that we had a problem: We waste valuable energy and time in conducting ineffective meetings. Having fingered the problem, we had to accept the fact that a dispute resolution process was necessary to restore the efficiency of the association. I think we recognized that, similar to training a horse, the problem needed to be solved using specific methods.

ETTA, however, is not accustomed to handling these types of problems and figured in time they would just go away (which, in my opinion, partially contributed to the problem). While we ranchers are not process oriented, the entire board was willing to gather prior to the regular meeting. We followed the CPR steps as they applied to our situation and personalities to allow us to focus on our specific needs. Paul and I both felt undue pressure heading what was commonly perceived as a "dysfunctional" board, so in addition to the ground rules, we sold the board on the idea to use a facilitator

We agreed that the process could feature a certain degree of flexibility; however, the board mutually decided that the facilitator may be internal to the association but must not be a member of the current board. As suggested in the CPR manual, we looked for a qualified but unbiased facilitator to work the group through its efficiency issues, allowing us to work as a team to overcome our problems.

The group requested the former board chair, Kelley, because of her facilitation training and known concern for the growth of the association. We asked her not to mediate but to guide the board through the CPR process. Not least among the benefits was that using a facilitator also relieved me and the CEO from our typical leadership responsibilities so that we could be a part of the group.

Step 1. Accept and activate awareness.

Having chosen a neutral facilitator, our group met prior to the regularly scheduled meeting. Kelley, the designated facilitator, announced that the first order of the meeting was to clarify the problem.

On a flipchart we listed the various issues impeding effective decision making during board meetings. Kelley reminded us to simply make a list without any finger-pointing. Paul and I began by expressing a few obstacles we had noticed, and collectively the board produced the following list:

- a lack of participation in decision making
- indifferent voting
- discussions dominated by the same few members
- dissatisfaction with membership benefits
- a general sense of favoritism shown to particular board members
- members pressuring others when voting
- long and tedious meetings
- the inconvenience of traveling to meetings
- a feeling that the group genuinely dislikes each other

After completing the list, Kelley assured the board that these types of problems are not unique to our association. We decided to take the next step, reminding ourselves of the purpose for holding this meeting.

Step 2. Aim.

Kelley pointed to the first and third ground rules posted on the wall: maintaining a dialogue with the intent of resolving our problems and focusing the meeting on the sole purpose of achieving more effective board meetings. She reminded us that our goal was to solve our efficiency problems and not to get caught up in personalities or emotions. She grinned and paraphrased Yogi Berra saying, "If you do not know where you're heading, you're likely to end up somewhere else."

Catching her enthusiasm, the board recognized that their perceptions and difficulties in making decisions affect the entire membership. Once we completed the difficult task of accepting and aiming we found it valuable to take each step separately.

Step 3: Acknowledge.

Setting a half-hour time limit, Kelley used our listed issues as a springboard for further dialogue. Although some of the problems listed seemed to occur secondarily, the board discovered what they thought was the primary issue: personal agendas. In other words, one member had established a power base, and all of the problems seemed to stem from that. As Kelley pointed out, that difficulty is seeing the problem as a group issue not blaming one person.

Mark, the member mentioned in the introduction who has a multistate operation, appeared to maintain a hold on the board because of the size of his organization. He not only has 12 members of ETTA within his company (triple the number of any other organization), but also due to his father and grandfather's involvement, his family has been members of ETTA since 1930. Mark had requested a weighted vote in board decisions, arguing that voting numbers should reflect the size of each rancher's business.

In addition, Mark's decision to use an alternate grain supplier negated the other members' ability to benefit from the association's group buying power. Immediately after the board meeting Mark announced that he needed to meet with staff ETTA and the CEO right now. A few of the members of the board were dismayed by Mark's private meeting and confused as to why he could not handle an additional issue during the meeting. The left-out board members anxiously assumed that Paul was persuaded to arrange the meeting locations to match Mark's travel schedule.

Since Mark's status and influence seemed to greatly affect the other board members, we decided that it negatively affected the way we worked together as a group.

After identifying the crux of the issue as self-interested power, we agreed to review how the problem directly affected the board and our ability to reach consensus. First, we carried out this step by looking at the issue objectively from all sides, as if the problem were in a cube. It seemed that Mark's attempt to manipulate power caused friction and resulted in a lack of willing participation for some members and open rebellion for other members who disagreed with Mark's stance and approach. Even though the issue focused on one individual, the group acknowledged that it actually affected the entire board, including the board chair and CEO.

Step 4. Seek accountability and address.

We asked ourselves: Who is accountable for our problems? Who must help us in initiating change and achieving our goals? Our initial, obvious answer was: Mark. However we quickly realized that the entire board withheld communication that would have helped us identify and confront our problems sooner. Mark is a vital member of ETTA and the board in particular, so we needed to find a way to use his valuable assets without compromising cohesiveness on the board.

During the open dialogue in the last few steps of the CPR process, the rumor surfaced that Paul and myself somehow shared Mark's interests and were favoring Mark over other members of the group, as evidenced by the corresponding meeting locations. Through the communication process, however, the rumor was quickly dispelled, as Mark explained that he requested the rotation schedule in advance so he could coordinate his business travel with our meetings.

Mark admitted that he was not aware that he had dominated the meetings and frustrated other board members. He confessed that his behavior is natural to his personality and that this character trait in conjunction with his experience in the business may come across as intimidating. "But how else can you be an effective horse breaker?" he teased, easing the tension in the meeting. Mark explained that he misread the other's silence as apathy, which made him all the more aggressive in expressing his views.

Sensing that the others were simply "filling the seats" and didn't care much about the meetings, he had suggested the weighted vote out of a conviction that he was contributing the most to the board anyway. Mark sincerely apologized for coming across as manipulative and self-interested. We believe he is simply passionate about the profession and, by his own admission, "comes from a long line of pushy know-it-alls." Mark promised that in future he would hold back a little so that the other board members could say and do more to participate.

With this new perspective, the board highlighted how Mark's experience and business associations benefited us but suggested he should recognize the best interest of the board and the larger association. Paul clarified, stating that the size and reputation of Mark's company is crucial in taking advantage of group buying power and Mark's choosing an alternate supplier drastically affected the group buying power.

Mark explained that a man from his hometown is his new supplier and is dependent on his business. He suggested that the entire association switch suppliers, assuring us that we could be offered a group rate comparable to that of the current supplier—if not lower. This, the board readily agreed, was in the best interest of the association.

Step 5. Award

Working through the CPR process, by now we had dispelled some critical misconceptions, confronted Mark about board perceptions, and achieved a better understanding of his personality and motivations. Now, we could reach consensus that a set of permanent ground rules for meetings as well should be drafted and implemented.

That task would give us a clearer sense of board members' roles, voting protocol, and responsibilities to association members.

We wrote detailed rules for future meetings using our current ground rules as a guide. Then it was easy to answer questions like: What should each of our regularly scheduled meetings accomplish? Who should participate? What are our motives?

The board secretary agreed to draft a document based on our suggestions and brought it to the next meeting for final approval and implementation. The board felt that the implementation of the CPR process, although uncomfortable at times, had been successful in smoothing out the process. As scheduled, the regular board meeting would commence after a welcome break for lunch. After a little mental recuperation, the participants were ready to tackle the regularly scheduled agenda items.

Paul gave each board member a clear plastic cube as a reminder to review the problem from hindsight, as a reflection on our earlier, "unlearned" behavior, in which we found ourselves rushing to place blame (which is not a part of the process) and then, having listed the problems, we attempted to rush into possible resolution.

Merely asking ourselves the questions about addressing and acknowledgement allowed us to move into step 5, award. We are mindful of the process. We added a ground rule that a board member can request a break from future board meetings to discuss an internal issue using CPR.

Appendix D
Case Study: The Wildlife Photographers Association

The Wildlife Photographers Association is seventy-five years old. A representative from each of the six regions is elected to serve on the board of directors, and the CEO maintains an office in Cheyenne, Wyoming.

Board members have experienced growing discontent in their board meetings for the past two years. Because this is a national organization, the 15-member board can convene only annually. The board leadership has a five-member executive committee consisting of the president, past president, first vice president, second vice president, and secretary treasurer. The executive committee convenes quarterly—more often if an emergency or particular issue dictates.

Change in the organization has been difficult to implement. For example, Cheyenne is not geographically convenient, but the organization started in Wyoming's capital, and resistance to change is stronger than the motivation of member convenience.

The CEO resigned a month ago, and a past president was selected to serve as the interim (salaried) CEO. As a footnote to the regular agenda for the upcoming board meeting, the interim CEO announced to the executive committee that they must set up a structure in which the CEO governs and the board is "subservient" (in the interim CEO's words). It seemed apparent that the interim CEO had jumped at the opportunity to make immediate changes to the association.

This development was, of course, controversial. Moreover, it generated discussion of a laundry list of issues confronting the association. For example, a side issue that surfaced resulted in pitting the executive committee members against two other board members. One executive committee member was concerned about board members who had become disengaged.

The governance issue generated a divisive argument over the association's direction, and the side issues stopped action on the scheduled agenda items.

The board decided to retain a facilitator, Francis, for a special meeting prior to the regularly scheduled meeting. A carefully crafted letter to each board member encouraged him or her to attend a one-day retreat immediately prior to the regularly scheduled meeting. The retreat, billed as a "board conditioning retreat," would focus on board operation as opposed to topics on the regular meeting agenda (for the next day). The package each board member received also included a sweatband and a workout towel to reinforce the theme.

More important, the letter of invitation included a brief survey, prepared by the facilitator and asking open-ended questions. In tabulation of the surveys, two additional items surfaced: a lack of trust of the executive committee and the intrusion of personal agendas by board members.

The retreat was scheduled for a suite at a local hotel, which for comfort had chairs arranged in a casual setting rather than the usual chairs at a square table. Two flipcharts completed the setup.

THE RETREAT

First, Francis, the facilitator, asked the group to establish ground rules, and he wrote those ground rules on a flipchart so they could be referenced throughout the process to foster group ownership. The group rules were:

1. Internal board issues will be the focus of the retreat. Regular agenda items will not be discussed but will be saved for the regular board meeting [that would take place the next day].
2. The meeting is confidential. Only by full concurrence of the participants will the discussion and results be disseminated to the membership at large.
3. A consensus model will be examined.
4. All board members are involved, and total participation is required.
5. We will agree to disagree and maintain respect for all opinions.
6. We are working on resolution—not winners or losers.
7. The facilitator will run the meeting. The CEO and board chair are equal participants.
8. We are working from facts, not emotions.

9. Issues will be prioritized for handling. It is agreed that all issues are important, but closure may not be reached in one day. Another retreat may be necessary.

COLLABORATIVE PROBLEM RESOLUTION (CPR)

By way of introduction, the facilitator said, "Photography is a step-by-step process, and no step has the same time frame for each shot. Some steps can be combined for some photos, keeping in mind that the components for success are structure, creativity, flexibility, and willingness to produce a better product. Well, this is also applicable to collaborative problem resolution."

Step 1. Accept and activate awareness.

Simple attendance at the board conditioning retreat activated step 1. The brief survey activated awareness of a problem. Francis used the CPR book to point out that problems on a board are not unique and to show the difference between discussion and dialogue.

At this point, the facilitator invited the group to identify six problems, concerns, and issues internal to the board and then prioritize them. Actually, nine issues emerged, and the group agreed to discuss all nine if possible, prioritizing them as follows:

1. Personal agendas. Board members seem to be on the board purely to enhance their own careers.
2. Some members refrain from participating.
3. The board does not have direction.
4. The board should determine qualifications for the new CEO prior to interviews.
5. Old members are quibbling with new members about the role of the association.
6. Governance: the role of the CEO and board.
7. Trust.
8. Changing the location of the office.
9. Resistance to change.

Recording these items on the flipchart accomplished step 1.

Francis reminded the group that this would be a tough process but the rewards would be high. To reinforce that idea, he placed a large box in the room containing assorted toys and candy. He promised that those offering comments that advanced the flow of dialogue would be rewarded with a trip to the "goody box." The group's skepticism was obvious until the first recipient scoured the box and found a favorite toy from childhood days.

Step 2. Aim.

Reviewing the list on the flipchart, Francis then asked, "What do we want?" and prepared to record the answers. Those who answered, "cohesiveness," "growth," and "adaptability to smooth the transition where change is needed" all received a trip to the goody box. Blaming was agreed not to be an option.

At this point, some issues prioritized in step 1 were combined, such as 3 and 5 and 8 and 9.

Step 3. Acknowledge.

Francis found that emotions, in favor of facts, were seeping into the discussion. So he reviewed the priority issues on the flipchart, and the group placed item 7, trust, at the top of the list. The facilitator proclaimed the importance of handling one issue at a time and moved directly to step 4 of CPR. He also assured the group that the entire list would be addressed once the new item 1, trust, had been handled.

Step 4. Seek accountability and address.

Everyone sees something a little different in the same photograph. For example, a change in lighting and a weed can appear a desert blossom. Francis explained that reframing is similar to looking at an object to be photographed from an entirely different angle. The brainstorming that followed included finding the origins of the trust issue.

Katrina, one board member, brought up the situation four years ago when the previous CEO was abruptly fired by the executive committee. She recalled that the entire board was involved in the selection process but that the chair alone made the decision to terminate the CEO. "What other strategic decisions," she asked, "were made and executed by the executive committee without the advance knowledge of the entire board?"

Francis reviewed the communication section on perceptions in the CPR book and asked for a brief roundtable, for the sharing of individual percepts that developed. Individual participants offered three perceptions about what had happened at that time:

1. The past board chair of four years ago assumed that all board members shared her feelings about the then-CEO's poor productivity, and she did not want to burden others or expose potential problems.

2. The then-CEO resigned out of a perception that the chair had sole authority to effect the termination and that the chair was displeased with his recent performance.

3. One member did become disengaged during the meetings held four years earlier because he was angered by other recent decisions and yet felt too threatened to offer a dissenting opinion. Despite his disengagement, however, he decided not to resign because he anticipated that things would improve.

As a result of the round table dialogue, members of the round table who also sit on the executive committee (five members of the board of directors) recognized the perception pitfalls. The executive committee members on the round table will return to the full executive committee with a recommendation to establish a communication process that adopts the principle of accountability to the board. The facilitator recommended ground rules for future meetings and a summary of agenda items and actions to be taken.

Step 5. Award.

The participants drafted an agreed-upon system for identifying the broad agenda items the executive committee may handle without communicating with the full board. They also agreed that the board would institute a newsletter to the full membership.

The issue of being disengaged was resolved by drafting ground rules for the regular board meetings. Francis explained that a board member should be able to remain silent on a particular issue without being considered as disengaged. However, ideally the chair would be able to occasionally step away from the regular agenda and ask if any problems might be likely to cause disengagement.

The board members congratulated each other on their efforts at resolving the first issue, trust, and consulted the flipchart for the next item.

Later on, the group discovered that item 3, disengagement, was resolved for the time being but monitoring would be necessary. Now that trust had been restored, it was recommended that the executive committee handle the governance issue during the next board meeting as the number one agenda item. This would also allow for research and idea formulation. The group agreed it would start the CPR process with the issue of changing the office location. But adaptability to change had to be dealt with first.

However, Francis recommended a break so participants could eat and refresh themselves and so he could replenish the goody box (even though, by now, fewer toys would be required because participants are combining more of the CPR steps to resolve the stated issues and are more comfortable with the CPR process).

Following the CPR steps gave the board participants the assurance that the group members would not jump to conclusions. They then collectively were confident that if they determined a headquarters move was necessary, they would not have to contend with a personal agenda being manipulated or worked by a board member such that the move would be for personal convenience.

BIBLIOGRAPHY

Fisher, A.B. *Perspectives on Human Communication.* Toronto: Macmillan, 1978.

Fisher, R., and Ury, W. *Getting to Yes.* Boston: Houghton Mifflin, 1981.

Hartman, T. *The Color Code.* New York: Fireside, 1998.

Hawkins, B., and Preston, P. *Managerial Communication.* Santa Monica, Calif.: Goodyear, 1981.

VISION STATEMENT

The ASAE Foundation will be the global leader enabling associations, their executives, and their partners to prepare for the future.

MISSION STATEMENT

The ASAE Foundation, in partnership with ASAE, is dedicated to enhancing the association community's ability to anticipate and prepare for change through education and research, thereby maximizing the community's positive impact on society.